There are over 100 subspecies of deer found all over the World, except in Antarctica.

Baby deer are called fawns, mothers are called does, and the fathers are called bucks, they are easy to find, they usually have horns, called antlers.

 **is for an Axis Deer.**

Axis deer are also called chital deer, and are found in India.

They are the most active in the early morning and late evening when it is cooler.

They live in herds (groups) of 10 - 30 deer.

My First Book about the Alphabet of Deer

Amazing Animal Books
Children's Picture Books

By Molly Davidson

Mendon Cottage Books

JD-Biz Publishing

Read More Amazing Animal Books

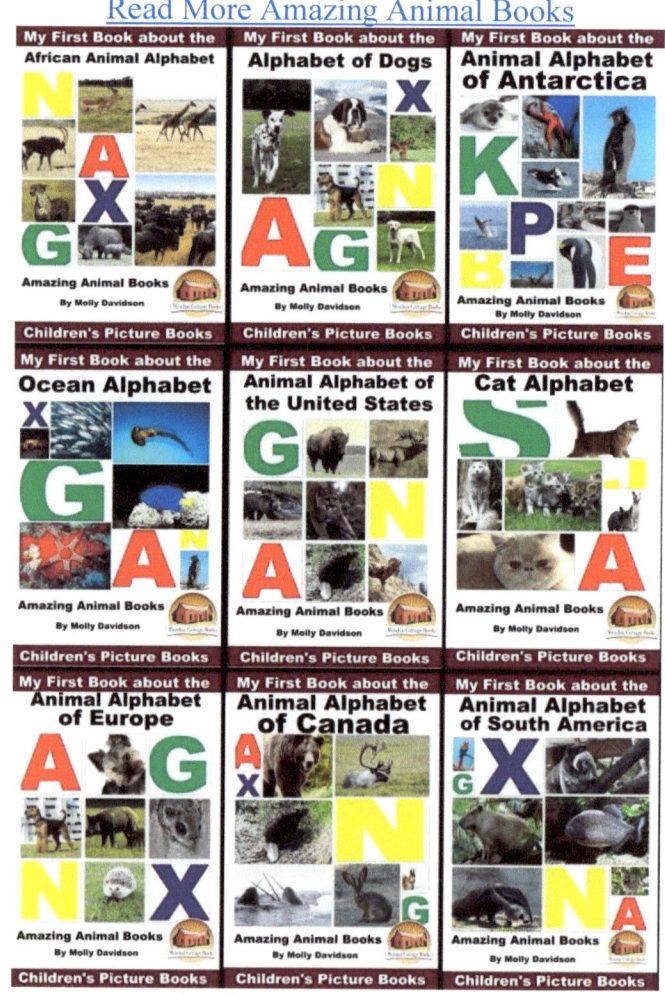

Purchase at Amazon.com
Download Free Books!
http://MendonCottageBooks.com

 **is for a Barasingha.**

Barasingha, also called swamp deer, live in India and Nepal.

They are known to have between 12 - 14 tines on their antlers; some have been seen with up to 20!

C is for a Caribou.

Caribou, also called reindeer live on the tundra of northern Canada, Alaska, Europe, Asia, and Greenland.

In the summer, they can eat up to 12 pounds of food (grass and plants) per day.

C is also for a Chinese Muntjac.

Chinese muntjacs have short antlers, less than 4 inches, which they use to push over predators, and then they hurt their predators with their two inch canine teeth.

They live in southeast China and Taiwan.

D is for a Dama dama, the scientific name for a Fallow Deer.

Fallow deer are found on almost every continent except Antarctica, living in herds of up to 150 deer.

 **is for an Elk.**

Elk are called wapiti by Native Americans, which means "light colored deer."

Boy elk, called bulls, lose their antlers every spring, and then grow them back in time for mating season in the fall.

E is also for Eld's Deer.

Eld's deer was named in honor of Lieutenant Percy Eld, a British officer.

They are listed as an endangered species, due to over hunting by humans.

They can be found mostly in Southeast Asia.

 is for Fea's Muntjac.

Fea's muntajcs are also called barking deer, because of the barking sound they make.

They are a rare species of muntjac, and only found in China, Laos, Vietnam, and Thailand.

They are named after a zoologist name Leonardo Fea.

G is for a Gray Brocket.

Dick Culbert © <u>Wikimedia Commons</u>

Gray brockets are found in South America, usually living by themselves.

H

is for a Hyelaphus Kuhlii, the scientific name for a Bawean Deer.

Midori © <u>Wikimedia Commons</u>

Bawean deer are a small deer standing about 2 feet tall, which live only on the island of Bawean in Indonesia.

I is for an Indian Hog Deer.

Indian hog deer live in the forests of Southeast Asia.

They run though the trees with their head down, ducking under tree branches instead of jumping over them like other deer.

 **is for a Javan Rusa.**

Javan rusa deer have large ears and eyes, much bigger than other deer with the same size head.

If they get scared, they will honk loudly to warn the others of danger.

They are very good at camouflaging within their habitat and are also very shy.

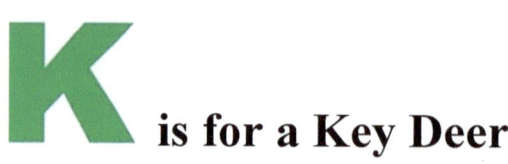 is for a Key Deer.

The key deer is an endangered subspecies of the white-tailed deer, which lives in the Florida Keys.

They eat more than 150 tropical plants and grasses, and drink freshwater from the wetlands.

M is for a Moose.

Moose are the largest animal in the deer species, weighing up to 1,800 pounds and standing over 6 feet tall.

Their antlers, also called spoons, can spread as wide as 6 feet from end to end.

 **is for a Northern Pudu.**

The northern pudu is the smallest deer in the World, standing about 14 inches tall.

They are found living on the Andes Mountains in Columbia, Peru, and Ecuador.

O is for an Odocoileus Hiemionus, the scientific name for a Mule Deer.

Mule deer get their name because of their ears, which are big like mules

They are found in groups of 3 or 4 all over the mountains of western North America.

P is for a Père David's Deer.

Père David's Deer are extinct in the wild, and are only found on animal preservers in China.

The boys have long tines on their antlers which point backwards.

They can live for up to 18 years.

R is for a Roe Deer.

Roe deer prefer to live in forests where they eat berries, grass, leaves, and tree shoots.

When it feels like it is in danger it will bark and show the white patch under its tail, helping to warn others of danger.

R is also for a Red Deer.

Red deer are one of the largest deer species, standing about 6 feet tall.

After the babies are born, the mothers will form large herds of up to 50 deer. The mothers help each other in protecting their babies from harm.

S **is for Sika Deer.**

Sika deer, also called the spotted or Japanese deer, live in the forests of East Asia.

They are about four times smarter than other deer, making them hard to hunt.

T is for a Tufted Deer.

Tufted deer are related to muntjacs, and also live in China and Myanmar.

They have a black tuft of hair on their forehead, which is where they got their name, and two tusks which can grow to be over 1 inch long.

T is also for a Taruca.

Chris Fryer © <u>Wikimedia Commons</u>

Taruca deer, also called north Andean deer, live on the rocky slopes of the Andes Mountains in South America

 **is for a Visayan Spotted Deer.**

D. Gordon E. Robertson © <u>Wikimedia Commons</u>

Visayan spotted deer are an endangered deer living on the Visayas islands of the Phillipines.

They are nocturnal, meaning active at night.

 **is for a White-Tailed Deer.**

White-tailed deer are the smallest deer living in North America.

They have a fluffy white hair patch under their tail, which they show to warn others of danger.

They can run up to 30 mph and leap as high as 10 feet.

W is also for a Water Deer.

William Warby © <u>Wikimedia Commons</u>

Water deer, also known as a vampire deer due to its long tusks, are found in China and Korea.

 **is for Yucatan Brown Brocket.**

Ricardo Jose Mena Baduy © <u>Wikimedia Commons</u>

The Yucatan Brown Brocket lives in tropical forests in the Yucatan Peninsula of Mexico.

They are nocturnal, active at night, and shy, so humans rarely see them.

Conclusion

I hope you have enjoyed reading this book about the amazing deer species.

One more fact, fawns, baby deer, take their first steps within half an hour of being born.

My First Book about the Alphabet of Deer

Horses
For Kids

Amazing Animal Books
For Young Readers
By John and
Annalee Davidson

Ponies
For Kids

Mendon Cottage Books

AmazingAnimalBooks
For Young R
Rachel Smith

Ten Amazing
Horses
For Kids

Nature Books for Kids
JD-Biz Publishing
K. Bennett

Akhal-Teke
"The Golden Horse
of the desert"
For Kids

Nature Books for Kids
JD-Biz Publishing
K. Bennett

Suffolk-Punch
"The Gentle Giant"
For Kids

Nature Books for Kids
JD-Biz Publishing
K. Bennett

Shires
"The great Horse"
For Kids

Nature Books for Kids
JD-Biz Publishing
K. Bennett

Colonial Spanish
"Horse of the Americas"
For Kids

Nature Books for Kids
JD-Biz Publishing
K. Bennett

Canadian
"The Little Iron Horse"
For Kids

Nature Books for Kids
JD-Biz Publishing
K. Bennett

Cleveland Bays
"History and Future"
Horses For Kids

Nature Books for Kids
JD-Biz Publishing
K. Bennett

Our books are available at

1. Amazon.com

2. Barnes and Noble

3. Itunes

4. Kobo

5. Smashwords

6. Google Play Books

Download Free Books!
http://MendonCottageBooks.com

Publisher

JD-Biz Corp

P O Box 374

Mendon, Utah 84325

http://www.jd-biz.com/

www.ingramcontent.com/pod-product-compliance
Lightning Source LLC
Chambersburg PA
CBHW050902290526
45792CB00002B/669